THE DON LANGUAGE

Powerful Insights of Excellence

KAUSHIK RAVIKUMAR

Clever Fox®
PUBLISHING

CLEVER FOX PUBLISHING
Chennai, India

Published by CLEVER FOX PUBLISHING 2025

Paperback ISBN: 978-93-6707-746-7
Hardback ISBN: 978-93-6707-390-2

Special Thanks to,

-M.R. Nagarathna (My loving Grandmother)
-B.R. Ravikumar (My supportive Father)
(Legal Advisor)

-Whoever helped me when I hit rock bottom
And to family and friends
Thanks to everyone I have met directly / indirectly
who has made me learn something.
Thanks to the power of language.

Dedicated to,

Whoever in this world is working to be excellent and Whoever likes to think.

-Hope this book of insights is valuable and helpful to you.

Note from the Author

This book is writen intentionally using as few words as possible because it is meant make you **think** more than it is meant to make you **read**.

This book of insights is through my lens and it is meant to help you find your own truth.

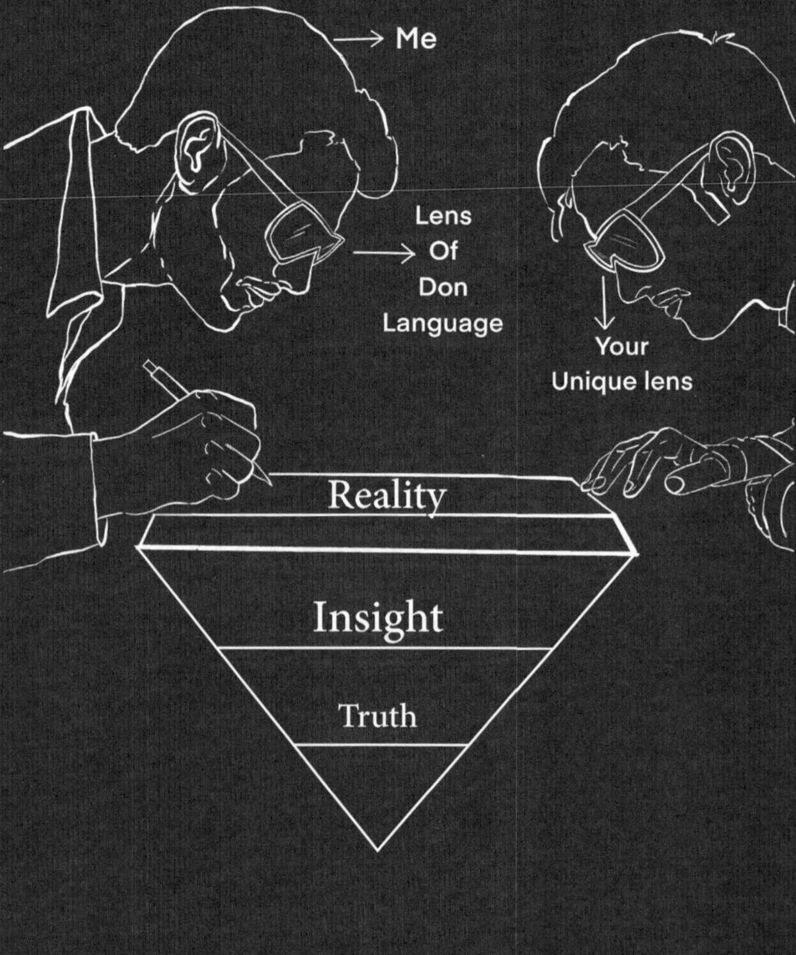

CONTENTS

CHAPTER 1

HOW TO BE POSITIVE AND BETTER

INTELLIGENCE:

YOU CAN WORK HARD YOUR WHOLE LIFE AND NOT BE SUCCESSFUL, OR YOU CAN WORK HARD USING THE RIGHT INFORMATION AND BE SUCCESSFUL FOR HALF OF THE EFFORT.

LOVE:

YOU CAN IDOLIZE AND FANTASIZE ABOUT LOVE, OR YOU CAN MOULD YOURSELF THE RIGHT WAY / PERFECTLY TO GIVE AND RECEIVE LOVE.

SELF:

YOU CAN SEARCH FOR ANSWERS / YOURSELF YOUR WHOLE LIFE AND NOT KNOW WHO YOU ARE, OR YOU CAN PLACE YOUR IDENTITY AS A GROUND ANYWHERE IN YOUR MIND, AND YOU CAN KEEP IMPROVING IT.

GOD:

YOU CAN PRAY TO AN EXTERNAL GOD, OR YOU CAN APPLY THE LESSONS OF GOD IN YOUR ACTIONS IN LIFE.

GROWTH:

A STAGNANT LIFE / A LIFE WITHOUT GROWTH MEANS YOU'RE DECAYING, BUT A LIFE WITH MOVEMENT AND GROWTH MEANS YOU'RE GETTING STRONGER TO FACE THE CHALLENGES OF LIFE.

HOW TO BE THE BEST:

EACH PERSON LIVES, BUT WHY ARE ONLY A FEW THE BEST AND FULFILLED WITH PEACE IN LIFE? DESPITE WHERE THEY HAVE COME FROM.

WHAT IN LIFE WILL SATISFY ME? AND WHY DOESN'T MY LIFE END EVEN WHEN I HAVE THAT? IS IT BECAUSE I WILL HAVE TO GO FOR MORE?

NEGATIVITY:

RIGHT / GOOD THINGS CAN TURN OUT TO BE BAD / WRONG. AND BAD THINGS CAN TURN OUT TO BE GOOD, WHICH MEANS I NEED TO KNOW WHAT THE ACTUAL RIGHT / WRONG THINGS IN THE WORLD ARE. BECAUSE THAT IS A BIGGER CHALLENGE THAN WALKING THE RIGHT PATH.

HOW TO NOT CARE:

I CAN CHASE EVERY LITTLE THING
IN THE WORLD, OR
I CAN HUNT WHAT IS IMPORTANT.

MISTAKES:

WHY SHOULD I EVER GO DOWN BECAUSE MY ACTION TURNED OUT TO BE A MISTAKE? IT MADE SENSE BEFORE THE ACTION. AND I WOULD CELEBRATE IF MY ACTION TURNED OUT TO BE BENEFICIAL. I CANNOT DO ANYTHING NOW EXCEPT TO LEARN FROM IT, AND GET BETTER.

HABITS:

BY EVERY SINGLE ACTION OF MINE, AM I TRYING TO GET SOMETHING / REACH A GOAL? OR AM I TRYING TO FEEL SOMETHING?

MONEY / WEALTH:

IF EVERY SINGLE ACTION OF MINE COSTS SOME SORT OF ENERGY / SOMETHING IN WEALTH, HOW CAN I NEVER RUN OUT OF THE ENERGY OF WEALTH TO LIVE MY LIFE?

WORK:

SHOULD I WORK TO SERVE 1000 PEOPLE, OR SHOULD I WORK TO SERVE BILLIONS? WHAT FULFILS ME?

RELATABLE:

I HAVE BEEN LISTENING TO PEOPLE MY WHOLE LIFE, AND I SPEAK TO SOME FROM WHAT I KNOW.

CHAPTER 2

INSPIRATION THROUGH INSIGHT

BEST:

IF I KNEW I WOULD DIE AT ANY MOMENT, I WOULD BE THE MOST SATISFIED WHEN I KEEP TAKING THE BEST ACTIONS IN THE "PRESENT MOMENT"-24X7. BECAUSE THERE IS NOTHING BETTER THAN THE BEST THAT I COULD DO.

GROWTH MINDSET:

I KNOW THAT I AM THE BEST, YOU CAN TELL ME WHY I'M NOT, I WILL ANALYZE IF THAT'S TRUE, THEN I'LL FIGURE OUT HOW TO GET BETTER AND BE THE BEST ANYWAYS.

NEGATIVES:

EVERY NEGATIVE THING IN THE WORLD IS TRYING TO MAKE ME GROW AND IS TRYING TO MAKE ME LEARN SOMETHING.

POSITIVITY IS A BETTER WAY TO LIVE. NEGATIVITY IS ANYTHING WHICH MAKES ME DIE MORE.

NOT CARING / PRIORITIES:

THERE IS CLOSE TO INFINITE NUMBER OF THOUGHTS / ACTIONS THAT I CAN TAKE. BUT MY TIME ON EARTH / LIFE IS LIMITED. SO, I SHOULD FOCUS ON WHAT IS IMPORTANT.

MISTAKES:

EVERY MISTAKE OF MINE, OR OTHERS IS JUST SHOWING ME WHAT THE RIGHT WAY / WRONG WAY TO LIVE IS. BY TRUTH AND NOTHING MORE THAN THAT.

HABITS:

I AM CONVINCED THAT EVERYTHING WE DO, WE DO IT TO FEEL SOME TYPE OF WAY OR TO BECOME SOMEONE WHICH MAKES US FEEL SOME TYPE OF WAY.

MONEY / WEALTH:

MY EXISTENCE IN THIS WORLD
DEMANDS THAT
I USE RESOURCES TO ACT IN IT. SO,
I NEED THE AMOUNT OF WEALTH
WHICH MAKES ME LIVE THE
WAY I NEED TO LIVE.

WORK:

WORK IS GIVING POSITIVE VALUE TO THE WORLD. SO, I NEED TO GIVE POSITIVE VALUE TO THE WORLD TO EARN THE VALUE I NEED TO LIVE MY LIFE.

RELATABLE:

I AM NOBODY COMPARED TO THE AMOUNT OF PEOPLE IN THE WORLD. BUT I CAN BE A SOMEBODY BY THE QUALITY OF THE PERSON I BECOME.

INTELLIGENCE:

THE INTELLIGENT / RATIONAL PART OF ME WORKS BY COPYING THE INFORMATION AND FACTS OF THE EXTERNAL WORLD INTO THE MIND.

INTELLIGENCE:

WHEN I HAVE TO BE MORE INTELLIGENT, I HAVE TO OBSERVE AND WORK WITH AS MANY PATTERNS IN THE WORLD. SUCCESSFUL INTELLIGENCE IS JUST OBSERVING AND WORKING WITH AS MANY PATTERNS OF TRUTHS OF THE WORLD.

EMOTIONS:

A GROUP OF FACTS, WHEN INTERPRETED AS A SINGLE THING BECOMES AN EMOTION.

EMOTIONS:

ALL OF THE EMOTIONS THAT WE FEEL ARE COMING FROM OUR PRIMAL EVOLUTIONARY BRAIN.

HOW TO BE POSITIVE:

I AM A NORMAL PERSON,
NEGATIVITY IS MAKING ME A KING,
HATERS ARE MAKING ME A GOD.

PEOPLE:

EACH PERSON IS A REFLECTION OF A PERMUTATION OF CHOICES OF HUMAN BEHAVIOUR.

LOVE:

ANYTHING THAT MAKES ME LIVE
MORE IS LOVE.

LOVE:

ANYTHING THAT MAKES ME LIVE MORE IS LOVE.

GOD:

MAYBE, JUST MAYBE, GOD IS NOT A PERSON, BUT A DISCOVERY OF THE WAY OF LIFE.

GOD:

THE ULTIMATE POSITIVE PATH IS GOD.

GOD:

IF GOD IS ULTIMATE POSITIVITY,
THEN HE / SHE WANTS EVERYONE IN
THE WORLD TO BE BETTER.

PREMISE TO LIVE YOUR LIFE:

"I CAN DO ANYTHING WHICH IS POSSIBLE IN THE REALITY'S STRUCTURE".

CHAPTER 3

MIND

External world

Processing mind

-- Focus

-- Emotions

-- Energy

-- Memories

-- Thoughts

-- Habits

-- Skill / Talent

-- Traits

-- Imprints

Processing mind:

It is a part of our mind that understands the world better. So that it learns lessons which can help us survive better.

Focus:

Focus is where our processing mind puts attention to, the external / internal, conscious mind / deeper parts of our mind.

For low focus, you have to see the area you need focus, as something important or create a sense of urgency, by see it as a mild form of threat.

Energy:

We get energy from the instinct of pain / pleasure, or the anticipated instinct of pain / pleasure.

Emotions:

Group of facts interpreted as a single thing is an emotion.

If we don't recognize the emotion, or where it's coming from, then its effect is amplified.

The type of emotions we feel is programmed in our primal evolutionary brain.
The awareness of emotions creates thoughts, and ignorance of thoughts creates emotions.

Memory:

Memory is unique information attached with high emotional intensity.

We can only remember information which is unique and with high emotional intensity and which is connected / (relevant) to the present moment.

Habit:

The pattern in which our thoughts / emotions / actions change through time is a habit.

Trait:

A Strong Habit with high intensity/ repetition is a trait.

Imprints / identity:

The part of ourselves (conscious / subconscious) which deeply makes us think / feel / act a certain way is an imprint / identity.

Observing mind:

The Observing mind is a higher level of awareness than our emotions. To reach this state, you should not act on any emotions / thoughts. Nor debate with it. You just have to observe whatever your mind is feeling / thinking. You can reach this state by meditating.

For negative emotions, you have to observe them and change the emotional trigger / the feeling to something positive.

Thought:

A single fact of information in the mind is a thought.

Talent is just a habit that is created and pushed into our subconscious mind.

A Skill is a group of habits working together for a common goal.

Trauma:

Trauma splits your personality and causes a negative imprint. The only way to solve it is to see the trauma as a thing of the past and not "The present", use whatever strategy to do this.

Deeper levels of pain require a deeper level of positivity / understanding to heal it. Solve it and you are powerful, or else you are stuck in pain being emotional your whole life.

What can go wrong in the mind?:

- You may have been imprinted with negative thoughts / emotions.
- Your emotions may be negative.
- You may have negative traits.
- You may struggle with focus.
- You may not be able to build skills.
- You may have low / high energy levels.

How to Deal:

Emotions are separate from the intelligence part of your mind.

Emotions are like a lens through which you see everything in the world.

Emotions have a trait of making us feel lost. So, we should raise our focus above the emotional level to just observe it, and not be influenced by it to make the emotion lose its effect.

Your intellectual part works by copying the information from external / internal sources into your mind.

- Different types where this works:
- Processing mind.
- Building skill / talent.
- Rational mind.

Whereas, all of our emotions are programmed in our evolutionary brain. And you can feel it based on your environment, which is perceived as fresh and relatable.

Emotion is helping us survive better by classifying many information as a simple feeling. But it can be deceived.

That is the reason we have to develop EQ (Emotional Quotient). You can intentionally trigger an emotion with the effort of the conscious mind.

Each emotion in you has a trigger for it to be activated, whether it's internal / from an external world.

The Most important ways your mind gets imprinted

- Genes
- Early childhood
- Emotionally intense situations

But you have more control over imprints than you think.

For habits:

You need to access the observing mind, and then get closer to the habit you want to adopt, starting with thoughts, emotions, and then actions.

If there are negative emotional imprints, then you need to heal resistances first, same as imprints.

Every emotion feels validated by the sense of 'Reward' it is receiving, and it tries to repeat the feeling to get the reward.

All emotions are created, held on and need to be released. When you feel an emotion strongly and you are unable to release that energy in the moment, when your mind doesn't see a resolution / release of that energy, it will find a temporary solution to not feel that emotion at that moment. In doing so, it locks that emotion as an imprint because it feels too intense (and by classifying that as important).

Because belief is an emotion, and it can overcome negative emotions when it is stronger than them. Passion (discipline) for something positive can work like belief. Because passion too is an emotion.

Or any other positive emotion can work as well.

Or by believing that you no longer need that imprint, or by believing and living in the present moment.

If you cannot believe / use emotion to remove a negative imprint. Then you have to go deeper to that negative imprint, understand what it truly wants through empathy for it to feel validated and worthy and to release that stuck emotion. You have to do it in a positive and healthy way.

If / when it is overwhelming , then you have to do this slow and steady.

You have to be true to yourself and empathize with all parts of you without judgment for it to work.

Stuck emotion / negative imprint can disguise itself as something else to our mind. That is why truth, empathy, and practically understanding it by testing it are necessary to heal it.

For high energy level:

You have to see the action of the present moment as less threatening or make yourself feel safe.

For low energy:

See the action of the present moment as a mild form of threat to create a sense of urgency. Or start being passionate about what you do, or by discipline. To see where you need more energy levels is important.

For skills / talent-see next chapter

For Negative imprints:

Each negative imprint is a locked emotion without the sense of time and space / place, which gets triggered by certain stimulus from external world / internal world.

The trick is to give that locked emotion a sense of what it wants by going deeper.

Tip:

Most stuck negative imprints come from fear, but can show up as something else on the surface.

EXAMPLE

On the surface	–	Addictive Behaviour
A Bit Deeper	–	"I want to have fun"
Recognising the emotion	–	"I want to have fun when I couldn't have fun". (Memory)
Recognising the Truth	–	"I can't have fun. Because it's so scary here. I want to run away".
Healing	–	"Oh, in the past, because it's not scary in the present moment".

Mastering emotions:

- An emotion becomes stronger the more you reward it.
- An emotion becomes weaker the less you reward it.
- It's the same for repressing an emotion. So it can be confusing.
- When the emotion accepts the release, it will not be repressed.
- When the emotion doesn't accept the release, then it will be repressed.

CHAPTER 4

HOW TO MASTER ANYTHING / ANY SKILL?

What is "the truth"?

The Truth is the same clear facts, which is powerful when acted upon.

The Truth is knowing the facts.

It feels clear and powerful, when acted upon the way of truth gives you success.

You can get confused with thoughts; you can get lost in emotions. Your actions may not give you results. But knowing / feeling / acting on the truth gives you clarity, power, and it gives fruitful results.

It doesn't matter if people around you / yourself majority of the people in the world are lost in confusions and illusions, but it is your job to find and work with facts to get powerful results. Because this is the road of mastery.

How to find the truth?

A statement ends a thought, and a question creates new ones.

Everything in the world has a structure.

Start from the goal and reason backwards from it to understand how you can reach it from your present situation.

GPS for finding the truth:

A neutral fact (not positive / negative) which can help you understand practically all of the opinions and emotions associated with it.

Example:

Opinion -1->All rich people are bad

Opinion -2->Rich people are not cultured like us

Opinion -3->You will be powerful when you're rich.

Opinion -4->Rich people break more rules.

The Truth: Money is powerful, but people who are rich are still human. They have the same emotions as everyone.

Because rich people don't have the same problems with money like poor people, they still have some sort of sufferings, just like every person in the world. Whether they are positive / negative with their personality, they are still human. Human emotions and human brain develop in them just like everyone in the world.

<u>SKILL MODEL:</u>

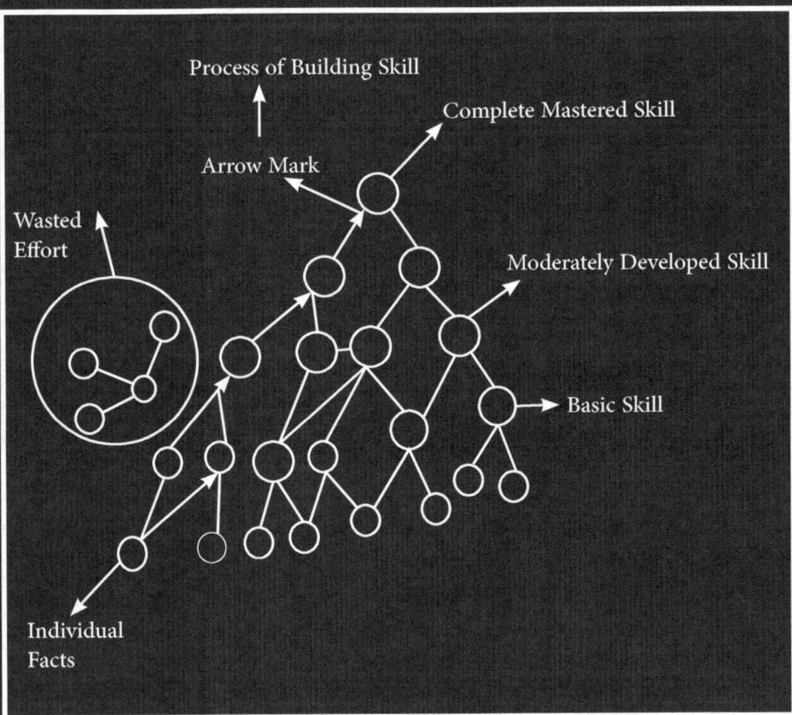

Skill Model Explanation:

It may consume more time and effort. Be prepared.

Start by observing the skill.

Find truths about the skill that you can keep improving and to re-align later.

Lay out all the information in front of you. And categorise and prioritize those information.

Break down the skill into smaller parts of habits.

Break down the habits of the skills into smaller habits, which you can build in the present moment.

Some of your perceptions of the truth and the habits of the skill may prove to be unproductive later. It is okay. Be prepared to improvise.

From the habits which you can develop in the present moment, You need to put effort and consciously build the habits.

Repetition and intensity of focus are important to make it strong.

Once that tiny habit is built, the trick is to connect it to the belief that you can perform that habit easily and confidently. Then performing of that habit becomes a deeper reflex coming from your sub-conscious mind.

So, now that tiny habit is built. Now, it's time to build another tiny habit using the same process.

After that, connect those tiny habits together using the same type of technique. (sub-consciously believing with confidence that you can perform those habits as a reflex).

Do not lose focus on the working of the skill. Use the Truth it is okay to realign with the truth. But stay clear on the Big-picture and stay clear on the way you need to go to connect big picture ideas with smaller details which you can apply in your present situation.

When your skill is moderately developed, you will gain confidence with this process, but the goal is mastery.

When you have reached the 'Mastery' level, you must stay focused.

Because you have built the whole skill with time and effort.

More you have perfectly executed the process of building tiny habits. More it's easier to gain confidence on 'Mastery' of that skill.

'Mastery' level requires strengthening tiny habits during practice and strengthening confidence in your skill in the present moment when you 'perform' that skill.

At the mastery level of the skill, you will be able to exactly understand what is going wrong / what is going right, How you can beat the competition, and how you can maintain this perception of the skill.

Mastering the skill is living in excellence.

At this level, focus only on what is important.

CHAPTER 5

HOW TO MASTER SKILLS (BY EXAMPLES)

A PERFECT "SELF-IDENTITY" IS FORMED BY ACCEPTING ALL PARTS OF YOU WITHOUT JUDGMENT USING EMPATHY, HAVING ROOM FOR GROWTH AND WHICH CAN COMPLETELY REGULATE YOURSELF BY SELF-AWARENESS.

Self:

Main reference is from "How the mind works"-chapter.

(On the surface)

↕

-- Thoughts
-- Actions / habits
-- Emotions
-- Belief systems
-- Identity / imprints

Deeper:

Actions:

Most obvious is to see where your energy is going in your everyday life.

High / low energy levels:

Regulate it / Heal it

Your emotional state:

Where you are / where are your emotional state is at the present moment, and how do you want it to be?

Heal it / connect it to slowly move towards your desired emotional state.

Imprints:

Heal it emotionally or a mix of analytical and emotional by going deeper.

Each imprint will have a belief system operating in your mind. It is easier to identify belief system then go even more deeper to identify imprints.

Your mind looks at everything internally and externally through the lens called "emotions".

To improve "intelligence": Indulge in "pattern recognition" of truth and applying it to the area where you want to be intelligent.

Tip:

There is always room for growth for intelligence and healthy emotions.

Thoughts:

Define healthy limits for your mind; certain triggers activate certain emotions / actions. Navigate your internal mind by clarity of your rational / analytical mind.

Identity:

You can search for answers of "Who you are" for your whole life / you can place your identity on certain emotions / actions / belief systems / traits imprint and improve from there.

Your sense of 'identity' is what is predictable for yourself. Heal resistance / conflicts.

Physical - Swimming

Mastery-perfect strokes with speed

- Strokes / actions
- Speed
- Physical fitness -> Training

  -> Nutrition

Habits for training and performing:

- Emotionally productive and healthy state 24x7.
- Growth mindset.
- The Right strategy and strength to build all their skills.
- Clear path / clear mindset to connect from where you are to get to mastery.
- To build every single habit till it's a reflex.

Emotional - Music Production

Emotional aspects:

- Focal element
- Sub-communication
- Harmony

Mastery:

To create tracks which give exactly the emotions that you need to give.

- Awareness of you / your brand
- Awareness of technical skills
- Awareness of emotions (to connect you and your technical skills to give the emotions you want)

Main Areas of Music Production:

- Sound design - "Who is speaking?" / instrumental.
- Composition – "What is the emotion?".
- Song structure – "What is the journey throughout the track?"
- Mix and master – "Technically implementing in the world of sound to give emotions".

Understanding the technicalities of music production and how it works emotionally. To give emotions that you / your brand wants to give.

Intellectual – Freestyle rap

Mastery – perform vocals powerfully to give the emotion that you want

Content

- Rhymes
- Setup-punchline
- Associations
- Sentence framing

Flow – sub-communicating (tone of voice)

Delivery

- You / brand awareness
- Technical awareness
- Emotional awareness

While performing

Mental flow

↓

Articulation

↑

Emotional state

- Build every single habit till it's a reflex.
- So that it's impactful while performing.

<u>While building:</u>

- Coming up with rhymes, association as a reflex.
- Thinking of the punchline first and the setup later as a reflex.
- Coming up with sentence framing as a reflex.
- Building technically and performing emotionally.

Strategy video game

DOTA-2

Mastery: To play the best moves with strategy in the game and win.

Main elements:

- **Hp**
  - Heal / Regen
  - Armour (physical)
  - Magic armour
  - Evade / Miss
  - Buff / Debuff
- **Mana**
  - Regen / Heal
  - Buff / Debuff
- **Damage**
  - Slow
  - Buff / Debuff
  - Physical
    - Pure
    - Cleave
    - Types of effect
  - Magical
    - Target / AOE
    - Types of effect
- **Agility**
- **Types of skills:**
  - Farming
  - Ganking
  - Pushing
  - Supporting
  - Drafting
- **Important factors**
  - Vision
  - Gold
  - EXP
  - ITEMS
- **Main Focus**
  - Timing
  - Positioning
  - Decision-making throughout the game.

"Every second of the game, with every action / click of the mouse / keyboard ->you are getting closer or further away from winning".

Practical - Business

Mastery-> To Be healthy and successfully be valuable internally and externally of the company.

All that matters is people

- Company / Brand
- Product / Service
- Consumers

- Employees
- Government
- Competition and other brands

(Measurement)

- Money
- Laws
- Information

Main focus-> Strategy

- H.R is managing employees.
- PR is managing the external people related to the company.
- Leading is taking the right decisions at the present situation of the company.
- Management is handling the people of the company effectively.
- Marketing is letting other people be aware of the product.
- Selling-> connecting your co / your brand to consumers through the product.
- Accounting is tracking the flow of money and resources inside and outside the company.
- Laws are measuring the structure of rules to be followed.

Measurement of a product / service:

- Pleasing / Value
- Unique
- Interesting
- Relatable

Mystery - FAME:

(And with more competition)

Mystery: To give what the audience wants through my product or service which is infused by my brand and fighting competition in the process.

- Me / Product / Service / My brand
- Other brands
- Competition
- Audience

How to execute:

- Place / events
- Media / social / media
- Contacts
- Merch
- Timing

CHAPTER 6

USEFUL INSIGHTS ON DIFFERENT AREAS OF LIFE

Chasing excellence every moment:

- Excellence is the best way to do something.
- Once you get there, you can still get better.

Body

Nutrition

- Carbohydrates
- Protein
- Fat
- Water

- Vitamins
- Minerals
- Fibre

Types of Exercises:

- Strengthening / Resistance
- Pressure
- Cardio
- Flexibility
- Balance

Money

- Earning
- Saving
- Spending
- Investing
- Strengthening
- Emergency / Retirement.

Investing:

- Saving
- Asset allocation
- Critical mass.

Safety Bucket

- Cash / cash equivalents
- Bonds
- C.D.
- Home
- Pension
- Annuities
- Insurance
- Structured notes

Growth Bucket:

- Equities
- High yield bonds
- Real Estate
- Commodities
- Currencies
- Collectibles
- Structured Notes.

Dream Bucket

Reference: Money: Master the Game -Tony Robbins

Best habits

- Waking up early
- Reading books
- Consuming great content
- Working out
- Working
- Meditating
- Discovery
- Recharging
- Reflecting

Success:

- Know who you are, Know what you want.
- Know your goal and things around it as much as possible.
- Take action towards the journey to reach your goal, improving on the way.
- Reach it. Celebrate and continue.

Wisdom

- You are right. Even if the other person / other idea is right.
- Find out how these things are true. And this belief system can bring you an abundance of knowledge and wisdom.

Thinking in the present moment

- Staying in the present moment by conscious awareness.
- Plan / prepare
- Execute
- Reflect on what happened and how you can get better.

- **Learning / growing yourself works like compound interest.**

Anything which helps you live more / better is wealth.

- Health, money
- Supportive people / social circle.
- Passion to move forward / get better.
- Healthy emotions
- Material things

Three levels of brain / mind:

Human brain

Mammalian brain

Reptilian brain

Perfect emotional regulation

- First deeply accept the rules to live / the best way to do something.
- Change your "present state" using an analytical mind / strong positive emotion by acting on the best thing.
- Indulge in it for a few moments, even though there is resistance emotionally.
- When you are out of your comfort zone, your resisting emotions will accept the present actions.

(If there is more resistance, it's because step 1 has not been executed perfectly.)

- Every single emotion / impulse of you wants something (in action / thought) to make itself feel like it is helping you survive better.
- Some emotions only help you in the short term, which can be unhealthy.
- It starts by negotiating, then, will slowly consume you / get itself into confusion to get what it wants. Stronger emotions always win. May / may not be deeper and / or positive.

Perfect way to change / build discipline

Step -1: Take the right actions.

Step -2: Create a sense of reward from those actions.

Repeat.

When the unproductive and unhealthy parts of you are too strong…it means…that it is feeling rewarded from your present (unhealthy / unproductive) actions.

To change this,

Focus on the healthy parts of you and create a sense of reward for them through your present actions, and deeply accept them.

Habits – Dopamine / reward patterns

Emotions – Changes in "lens" through triggers

Energy / impulses – Your sense of threat / pleasure patterns.

Hacking Dopamine / Reward patterns:

You feel rewarded by

- Winning challenges
- Doing difficult things successfully
- Fighting resistance successfully.

Love – (for men)

- Love has a structure
- Most types of love are conditional

- Communication
- Passion / attraction
- Emotions
- Lifestyle

A girl / woman's natural state is being emotional.

But what attracts her to you are passion / masculine traits (traits of you that indicate that you are surviving better in this world)

Things like:

- Your drive to succeed.
- Your achieved successes.
- Your physical attractiveness.
- How you maintain relationships.

(These creates interest in the girl)

But when you want to attract a girl for the long term. What's important is your "lifestyle".

Too much passion without a lifestyle attracts her in the short term.

Without passion / attractiveness, you are in the friendzone / brozone.

Communication is how you convey attractiveness, your emotions and your lifestyle in the best and healthy way.

All the types of your emotions don't matter to attracting the girl; only the type of emotions which serve the purpose of attracting and keeping the girl matters.

Girls need empathy more than you think

Habits / lifestyle	↑	On the surface
Emotions	│	
Belief system	│	
Imprints / identity	↓	Deeper

Apply it to match your world to the world of the girl you are trying to attract.

Love (for women)

- Love has a structure
- Most types of love are conditional
- Communication
- Passion / attraction
- Emotions
- Lifestyle

The natural state of a man is passion / movement.

What attracts a man / guy to you is, your talents / abilities to nurture life.

- It may be looks
- It may be traits
- It may be your belief system (on a deeper level)

When you want to attract a guy for the short-term, you can show these traits on the surface and may be a little deeper.

When you want to attract a guy for long term, you have to make sure that the guy understands, recognises and validates deeper parts of these traits healthily.

Guys / men need communication more than you think.

When a guy is attractive but is emotional around you, it's because he doesn't know what's attractive about him to you, and he is emotionally stuck somewhere.

But most attractive guys want to understand how to get better and treat you better.

So, you can establish healthy positive boundaries for his behaviour around you through communication and empathy to keep the attraction and the relationship strong.

Habit / lifestyle	↑	On the surface
Emotions	│	
Belief System	│	
Imprints / identity	↓	Deeper

Match your world to his for the relationship to work.

Guys / men may not feel how you feel, but they can understand most of the time.

Guys / men are emotional only in a few areas of their lives.

Measuring factors while dealing with other people.

Observe:

Habit / Lifestyle	↑	On the surface
Emotions	│	
Belief System	│	
Imprints / identity	↓	Deeper

Observe yourself and other people to match your elements with other people. It may not be the same, but it has to complement each other.

CHAPTER 7

SOCIAL INTELLIGENCE

HOW GREAT YOU ARE IS EQUALLY IMPORTANT AS HOW YOU TREAT YOURSELF AND OTHER PEOPLE.

YOU CAN BE THE GREATEST PERSON IN THE WHOLE WORLD, AND YOU DON'T HAVE TO TELL THAT TO OTHER PEOPLE.

YOU CAN GIVE WORLD CLASS-
INFORMATION TO PEOPLE, BUT
THEY WILL ONLY UNDERSTAND IT
FROM A POINT WHERE THEY ARE OR
WHICH MAKES SENSE TO THEM.

PEOPLE WILL SHOW YOU HOW THEY FEEL ABOUT YOU AND NOT ALWAYS SAY IT.

EVERYONE IS TRYING TO SURVIVE IN THIS WORLD, AND IF YOU SHOW THAT YOU ARE BETTER THAN THEM, EVEN IN A SLIGHTLY NEGATIVE WAY, THEY WILL SEE YOU AS COMPETITION.

YOU CAN'T DO ANYTHING FOR PEOPLE WHO HATE YOU JUST BECAUSE YOU'RE BETTER. BECAUSE THAT IS TRIGGERING THEIR INSECURITIES.

DISTANCE YOURSELF FROM PEOPLE WITH WHOM YOU CAN'T HAVE A POSITIVE, HEALTHY RELATIONSHIPS. BUT SHOW UP IN THEIR LIFE REGULARLY AND JUST GIVE POSITIVITY WITHOUT EXPECTING ANYTHING, WE ARE NOTHING WITHOUT PEOPLE.

IF SOMEONE HAS TREATED YOU BADLY, IT'S BECAUSE YOU WERE NOT ABLE TO ESTABLISH BOUNDARIES TO PROTECT YOURSELF.

IF SOMEONE HAS HURT YOU BADLY, YOU CAN TAKE REVENGE BY HURTING THEM. BUT HOW WILL YOU TAKE REVENGE ON THE MEMORIES OF THEM IN YOUR MIND? SIMPLE, FORGIVE WITH EMPATHY AND FORGET.

LEARN FROM THOSE WHO ARE BETTER THAN YOU. TEACH THOSE WHO ARE BELOW YOU. BEFRIEND HEALTHY PEOPLE EQUAL TO YOU. NOT JUST BY WORDS, BUT BY EMOTIONS AND ACTIONS.

IF YOU HAVE BEEN FRIENDS WITH SOMEONE FOR 20 YEARS. AND YOUR RELATIONSHIP WITH THEM IS GETTING NEGATIVE BEYOND REPAIR. IT IS TIME TO CUT THEM OFF.

IT IS OKAY IF PEOPLE WERE HURTING YOU WHEN YOU WERE POWERLESS. FIND A WAY TO BE POWERFUL AND CUT THEM OFF TO PROTECT YOURSELF.

WHEN FEW PEOPLE AROUND YOU ARE NOT GETTING ENVIOUS, THEN YOU ARE NOT BECOMING GREAT BY PUSHING YOUR LIMITS.

EVERYONE IN THE WORLD DO NOT NEED SUCCESS; SOME JUST WANT LOVE. SOME WANT PEACE, AND SOME JUST WANT TO EXIST.

IT DOESN'T MATTER WHAT PEOPLE HAVE DONE TO YOU. IT ONLY MATTERS HOW YOU TREAT THEM AND MORE IMPORTANTLY WHAT MATTERS IS HOW YOU TREAT YOURSELF.

PEOPLE ARE MANY, AND THEIR SITUATIONS ARE MANY. THOSE ARE DETAILS, BUT EVERYONE IS GOVERNED BY THE SAME HUMAN EMOTIONS.

PAIN<->PLEASURE (ENERGY)
HAPPY<->SAD
ANGER<->FEAR
CALM<->OVERWHELMED

These are opposite emotions. Use it to relate with people positively. Be formless.

FAMILY:

LOVE AND LOYALTY ARE MORE IMPORTANT TO FAMILY THAN ANYTHING ELSE.

SIBLINGS:

WHEN YOUR PERSONALITIES MATCH, OR WHEN THEY DON'T, YOU CAN HAVE HEALTHY RELATIONSHIPS WITH EVERYONE IN THE FAMILY AS LONG AS THERE IS RESPECT FROM EMPATHY AND HEALTHY BOUNDARIES.

FRIEND:

YOU CAN'T ALWAYS GET THE FRIEND YOU WANT, BUT YOU CAN ALWAYS ACCEPT THE FRIEND YOU GET.

FRIEND:

TELL ME, DO YOU WANT INCREDIBLE SUCCESS BUT LONELINESS FOR THE REST OF YOUR LIFE? OR DO YOU WANT SUCCESS AND HAPPINESS WITH A FEW CLOSE FRIENDS?

EXTENDED FAMILY:

WHOEVER CAME TO SEE YOU WITH POSITIVITY. THEY SPENT TIME AND EFFORT TO DO IT. RESPECT IT.

COMMUNITY:

YOU GET INSIDE A COMMUNITY BECAUSE OF SHARED VALUES AND SHARED TYPES OF BEHAVIOUR. TO MAINTAIN IT SHOULD BE YOUR PRIORITY. IF YOU CAN'T, THEN ITS BETTER TO LEAVE THAT COMMUNITY.

SOCIAL GROUPS:

BE A BIRD WITH BIRDS, A SHARK WITH SHARKS, AND A LION WITH THE 'PRIDE'. BUT DON'T TRY TO BE ALL AT ONCE.

CITY / STATE:

NO MATTER HOW BAD / GOOD IT WAS, YOUR LOCAL CULTURE / CITY KEPT YOU ALIVE AND SHAPED YOU INTO AS YOU ARE NOW. YOU OWE IT MORE LOVE, THE GREATER PERSON YOU BECOME.

COUNTRY:

HATE ONLY GETS YOU HATED.
ACCEPT YOUR FAMILY, FRIENDS,
COMMUNITY / COUNTRY
UNCONDITIONALLY.

WHOLE WORLD:

EACH PERSON IN THE WORLD DIRECTLY / INDIRECTLY IMPACTS YOUR LIFE. EACH PERSON IN THE WORLD HAS THEIR OWN LITTLE WORLD FROM WHICH YOU CAN LEARN / GET BETTER.

IT DOESN'T MATTER WHAT MISTAKES YOU MADE, IT DOESN'T MATTER HOW BAD IT WAS. THE ONLY THING THAT MATTERS IS HOW YOU LEARN AND GET BETTER FROM IT, UNTIL YOU HAVE BREATH IN YOUR BODY.

CHAPTER 8

HOW TO LEAD

THINKERS KNOW THE WAY. LEADERS WALK THE WAY.

WHEN PEOPLE HAVE THE POWER OF LEADERSHIP…NEGATIVE LEADERS MAKE PEOPLE JUMP OFF A CLIFF, MAKE PEOPLE DROWN IN THE OCEAN, BURN IN FIRE AND MAKE PEOPLE GET LOST IN EMOTIONS AND ILLUSIONS. POSITIVE LEADERS PROVIDE CLARITY, TRUTH, MAKE PEOPLE CLIMB MOUNTAINS, HELP PEOPLE SOLVE THEIR PROBLEMS AND HELP NAVIGATE THE WORLD BETTER.

YOU ARE JUST A NORMAL PERSON LIKE EVERYBODY ELSE. WHAT MAKES YOU THINK THAT YOU CAN LEAD OTHER PEOPLE? IF YOU WANT TO LEAD, PEOPLE MUST TRUST YOUR ABILITIES, PRACTICAL TRUTH THAT YOU HAVE AND EMOTIONAL CONFIDENCE THAT YOU POSSESS, WHICH ONLY COMES FROM PROVING YOUR ABILITIES AND PRACTICAL TRUTHS IN YOUR OWN LIFE.

WHEN YOU KNOW THAT YOU ARE THE BEST AND YOU ARE LIVING THE MOST POSITIVE, HEALTHY, ABUNDANT LIFE, AND YOU KNOW ANYONE CAN HAVE THE LIFESTYLE OF YOURS PRACTICALLY, THEN EVERYONE IN WORLD NATURALLY WANTS TO FOLLOW YOU.

THE ELEMENT OF LEADERS IS ALWAYS THE SAME, WHETHER IT'S PAST, PRESENT / FUTURE. THEY JUST MAKE POSITIVE KNOWLEDGE AND WISDOM RELATABLE TO THE PRESENT MOMENT.

THE LACK OF RELATABILITY OF POSITIVITY IN THE PRESENT MOMENT MAKES PEOPLE LIVE MORE IN AN EMOTIONAL / ANIMALISTIC STATE (OUR NATURAL STATE). WHICH CAN BE NEGATIVE. THUS, BIGGER AND MORE RELATABLE LEADERS ARE REQUIRED FOR EVERY GENERATION.

HAVING THE KNOWLEDGE, WISDOM AND SUCCESS IN YOUR OWN LIFE DOES NOT GUARANTEE YOUR LEADERSHIP ABILITIES. WHAT GUARANTEES IS YOUR ABILITY TO MAKE THE WISDOM EASILY RELATABLE TO OTHER PEOPLE THROUGH EMPATHY.

YOU CAN BE AT LEVEL 10 / 10, BUT HOW WILL YOU LEAD A PERSON WHO IS INNOCENTLY AT 3 / 10 ? YOU HAVE TO THINK, FEEL AND ACT IN A WAY WHICH MAKES OTHER PEOPLE UNDERSTAND YOUR TRUTH. IN SIMPLE TERMS, LEADING IS MORE ABOUT OTHER PEOPLE THAN IT IS ABOUT YOURSELF.

WHEN YOU HAVE EXCEPTIONAL ABILITIES AND POWER, IT IS YOUR DUTY TO LEAD OTHER PEOPLE. IT IS NOT A SOLO GAME. HUMANITY IS A COLLECTIVE GAME.

IF YOU ARE SUCCESSFUL AND POWERFUL BUT DON'T KNOW HOW TO LEAD OTHERS, IT IS BECAUSE...

YOU DON'T KNOW HOW POSITIVITY AND SUCCESS WORK PRACTICALLY IN A WAY THAT YOUR STRATEGIES CAN BE REPLICATED.

AND / OR:

YOU DON'T HAVE EMPATHY TOWARDS OTHER PEOPLE.

BEING AGGRESSIVE DOESN'T MEAN THAT YOU ARE THE BEST, NOR DOES IT GUARANTEE SUCCESS IN LEADERSHIP. GIVING THE EXACT VALUE WHICH PEOPLE NEED TO LIVE THE BEST LIFE GIVES YOU SUCCESS. SOMETIMES IT MAY BE AGGRESSION, SOMETIMES CALMNESS, LOVE, OR SOMETIMES BEING STERN. LOVE AND POSITIVITY COME IN DIFFERENT TRAITS AND EMOTIONS.

IF YOU WANT TO LEAD, THEN LEAD
AN INTENTIONAL LIFE.

NOBODY WANTS A CONFUSED
LEADER OR A LEADER WHO IS LOST.
RATHER, THEY NEED A LEADER
WHO IS CLEAR IN HIS HEAD, CALM
AND CONFIDENT IN HIS HEART AND
PURE IN HIS SOUL.

IF YOU MAKE MISTAKES WHEN LEADING, YOU ARE RISKING YOURSELF AND THE LIVES OF OTHER PEOPLE. BE PREPARED BEFORE YOU LEAD, AND HAVE A STRATEGY TO DEAL WITH MAKING UNCONTROLLED MISTAKES WHILE LEADING.

YOUR OWN UNIQUENESS MUST COME THROUGH WHILE LEADING YOURSELF AND OTHERS. AT THE SAME TIME, YOU HAVE TO BE FLEXIBLE TO ADAPT TO YOUR CURRENT SITUATION.

IF PEOPLE HATE YOU, YOUR LEADERSHIP, AND IF IT'S BECAUSE OF ENVY, THEN IT'S BECAUSE YOU ARE UNRELATABLE, OR YOU ARE MAKING MISTAKES.

IF PEOPLE ARE MORE ENVIOUS OF YOU THAN THEY ADMIRE YOU, THEN YOU HAVE TO PROVE YOUR ABILITIES BY GETTING BETTER / SUCCESSFUL. TO MAKE THEM COMFORTABLE, AND TO MAKE THEM TRUST THE POWER YOU ARE HOLDING WILL NOT HURT THEM.

SOME HATE COMES FROM INSECURITIES, STUBBORNNESS, AND IGNORANCE; YOU CANNOT WIN IN THOSE SITUATIONS. BETTER TO AVOID AND IGNORE THOSE TYPES OF PEOPLE, SITUATIONS AND FOCUS ON IMPROVING THE LIVES OF PEOPLE WHO TRUST YOU.

NO MATTER HOW BETTER YOU GET,
SOME PEOPLE CANNOT FORGIVE
AND FORGET THE MISTAKES YOU
MADE WHEN YOU WERE WEAK.
TAKE MORE TIME AND APPLY
EMPATHY TO THEM TO MAKE THEM
TRUST YOU AGAIN.

WHEN YOU ARE A LEADER, EVERY GRAND VISION TO EVERY TINY DETAIL WILL BE JUDGED, AND IT IS IMPORTANT TO SHOW UP AS YOU WANT TO BE PERCEIVED. OR AN EASY WAY IS TO BE CLEAR AND HONEST WITH YOUR STRATEGIES.

VALUE ATTRACTS. EMPTINESS / NEEDINESS CHASES.

A GREAT LEADER LEADS PEOPLE WHO ARE ABOVE THEM, PEOPLE EQUAL TO THEM AND PEOPLE WHO ARE BELOW THEM.

WHEN YOUR STRATEGY / PHILOSOPHY FOR ATTAINING SUCCESS IS THE BEST IN ONE ARENA, THE SAME POSITIVE WISDOM IS RELATABLE FOR PEOPLE IN OTHER AREAS OF LIFE, BECAUSE THEY CAN SENSE YOUR SPIRIT MORE THAN THEY CAN SENSE YOUR TECHNICAL ABILITIES.

YOURSELF:

TO LEAD YOURSELF:

BE COMPLETELY SELF-AWARE.
(INCLUDING STRENGTHS AND
WEAKNESSES)
BE CLEAR ABOUT YOUR WAY
THEN WALK YOUR WAY.

MIND:

THOUGHTS CAN BE ABUNDANT AND CONFUSING, EMOTIONS CAN BE MANY AND OVERWHELMING, AND ACTIONS MAY BE DRAINING. BUT WHEN YOUR METHODS OF REGULATING YOUR MIND ARE STRONG, THEN YOU HAVE MORE CONTROL OVER YOUR MIND.

EMOTIONS:

EMOTIONS ARE SPARKED, THEY NEED SOMETHING, AND THEN THEY LET THEMSELVES GO. USE THIS FLOW OF EMOTIONAL ENERGY POSITIVELY AND PRODUCTIVELY.

FAMILY:

WHAT YOU SAY TO YOUR FAMILY IS EQUALLY IMPORTANT AS HOW YOU SAY IT AND HOW THEY PERCEIVE IT.

SIBLINGS:

LEADING YOUR FAMILY IS BUILT MORE ON TRUST AND ACCEPTANCE THAN ON YOUR RATIONAL ABILITIES.

FRIENDS:

LEAD PEOPLE WHO WANT TO BECOME POWERFUL. HELP PEOPLE WHEN THEY NEED IT. BUT DON'T JUST GIVE OUT FREE MEALS AND MAKE PEOPLE DEPENDANT ON YOU. BE FRIENDS WITH THOSE WHO ARE POSITIVE AND HEALTHY.

MIND AND DECISION MAKING:

WHEN YOU CARE ABOUT SOMETHING, YOU GET CLOUDED BY EMOTIONS.

WHEN YOU CARE ABOUT FACTS WITH CONSISTENT PROOF, IT BECOMES YOUR TALENT.

LEAD PEOPLE:

A MAGICIAN SHOCKS THE CROWD,
AND A LEADER WITH MAGIC TRICKS
BECOMES A "GOD".

EXTENDED FAMILY:

BEFORE TALKING, FEELING AND ACTING, KNOW AT WHICH LEVEL PEOPLE ARE, AND THEN ACT IN A WAY THAT THEY UNDERSTAND.

COMMUNITY:

BE FAMILIAR AND PREDICTABLE WITH YOUR COMMUNITY; ACTING TOO MUCH OUT OF CHARACTER WITH THEM MEANS LOSING THEIR TRUST.

SOCIAL GROUPS:

GIVE MORE THAN EXPECTED VALUE TO PEOPLE TO MAKE THEM TRUST YOU, GIVE EQUAL VALUE AS EXPECTED FROM YOU TO BE COLD / TO DISTANCE YOURSELF.

CITY / STATE:

ACTING TOO MUCH AGAINST YOUR REGIONAL / CULTURAL SOCIETY THAN EXPECTED WILL GET YOU HATE OR MAKE YOU GET CAST ASIDE.

COUNTRY:

HAVE GRAND VISIONS, BUT MAKE THEM RELATABLE TO THE PEOPLE YOU ARE LEADING IN THE PRESENT MOMENT.

SHOW PEOPLE WHERE THEY SHOULD GO RATHER THAN TELLING THEM WHERE NOT TO GO, AND WHAT NOT TO DO. WE NEED LOVE MORE THAN WE NEED FEAR.

PLACE:

BE A BEGGAR IN THE SLUMS, AND A KING ON THE THRONE. BUT NEVER LOSE RESPECT FROM OTHERS OR FOR YOURSELF WHEN YOU ARE ALONE.

TIMING:

NEGATIVITY TAKES THE PATH OF LEAST RESISTANCE. THE PATH OF SHORTCUTS. BUT POSITIVITY TAKES THE RIGHT TIME TO GET THERE.

SITUATIONS:

NO TYPE OF SITUATION CAN SHOCK YOU WHEN YOU ARE AWARE OF YOURSELF, YOUR PATH AND YOUR STRATEGIES, BUT WHEN YOU TAKE A LOSS; IT'S TIME TO LEARN / GROW.

IT IS BETTER TO OVER PREPARE PRACTICALLY THAN TO BE CAUGHT OFF-GUARD.

POSITIVE / GOD:

GOD IS THE ULTIMATE POSITIVE PATH. HE / SHE WANTS EVERYONE TO BE AS POSITIVE AS THEY CAN BE. WHEN YOUR SPIRIT IS POSITIVE. YOU ARE HELPING TO INCREASE POSITIVITY IN THE WORLD.

CHAPTER 9

SPIRITUALITY

Based on Belief.

Not scientifically proven yet.

- I may be wrong with a few contents in this chapter, but one day science won't be.
- Humanity will see massive progress when we find a way to measure "The Mind" and "The Emotions".
- Everything in this world has a structure, and we may not understand it right now. Doesn't mean the structure is not there.
- Anything that makes us live more is love.
- Anything that makes us live better is positivity.
- Anything that kills you more is negativity.
- God is the ultimate positivity / ultimate positive path.
- The Structure of the path of God, love and spirituality may not be proven yet. But having a reference point of those beliefs parallel to practicality and structure can help you learn and grow tremendously (instead of dismissing it with ignorance, even if you don't believe it).

Combining Basic Human Emotions and Traits of Planets intuitively:

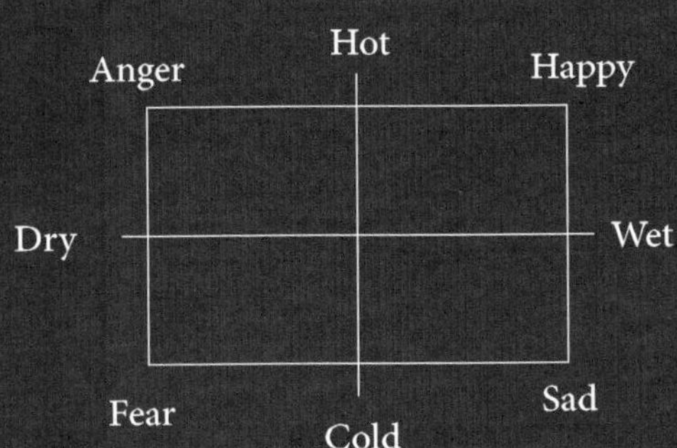

- Every element / every living / non living thing in the world is a combination of one or more of these elements.
- Every measuring element Humans have created / discovered is influenced by replicating / measuring things in nature / the external / internal world.

Measuring factors of the world:

- Numbers (Maths, calculations, measurement of forces)
- Time - (Hours, days, years, etc…)
- Space (Distances, areas, etc…)
- Elements-(Nature, chemistry, things, people, etc…)
- Alphabets - (letters, words, sentences useful for communication, colour, sounds, etc.)

Intuitively observing physical characteristics of the world

- Physical actions -> Movement – Fire
- Stillness in action -> Stagnancy – Earth
- Thought and mind -> Communication / Intelligence – Air
- Group of facts interpreted as a single thing -> Emotions -Water

<u>Astrology / birth chart:</u>

- Planets- What is happening?
- Houses- Where / which area of life?
- Sign- How is it affecting?

Types of houses / signs:

- Fire →
- Earth →
- Air →
- Water →

Sub - Division →

- Start / Cardinal
- Fixed
- Mutable / Changeable

Types of planets / elements made up of

- Sun - Hot-(Shining, Identity)
- Moon- Wet-(Emotional)
- Mercury- Dry / Wet-(Quick, Changeable Temperament)
- Venus- Wet and Hot (Love and Luxury)
- Mars- Hot and Dry (Fighting / Aggressive)
- Jupiter- Hot and Wet (Expansion)
- Saturn- Cold and Dry (Strict)
- Uranus- Cold and Dry (Unpredictable)
- Neptune- Cold and Wet (Dreamy)

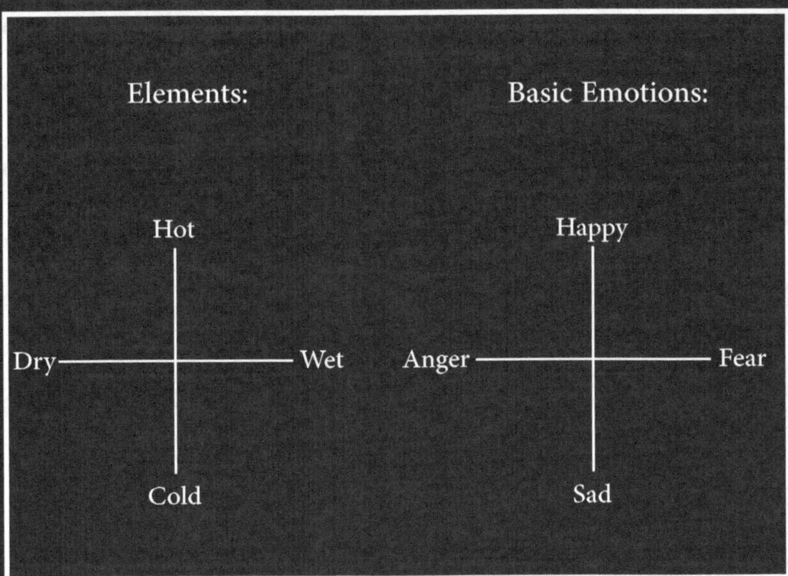

Intuitively understanding numbers:

0 – Nothingness.

1 – Body / Identity -> Sun.

2 – Internal / External World / Partnership -> Moon.

3 – Social / Expansion -> Jupiter.

4 – Stability (House) or Eccentric -> Rahu / Uranus

5 – Movement / Change -> Mercury

6 – Harmony / Love -> Venus

7 – spiritual / Knowledge -> Neptune / Ketu

8 – Structure / Infinity -> Saturn

9 - Aggression / Reflection of Energies -> Mars.

If a group of facts interpreted as a single thing is called as "emotions". Then, group of traits / energies interpreted as a single thing is a "Name", and the total numbers of your birth date.

The frequency of numbers and how it affects us in the world may not be scientifically proven yet. But the fact that it is accurate some of the time makes it worthy of exploration.

Measuring Free Will:

1. Structure (Different Areas of life) (Family, Career etc.,)

2. Frequency (Type of Color)

3. Positive / Negative (Dark / Light Color)

4. Intensity (Line of Intensity)

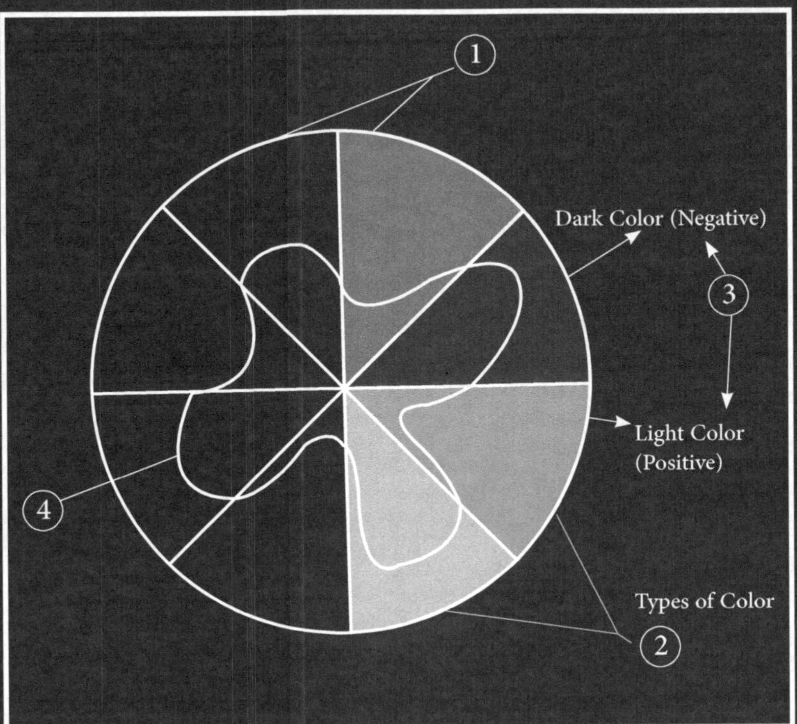

- The Range of frequencies / energies is like different emotions we feel.
- **Structure is what the areas of life are:**
    - Sports(/ Physical)
    - Meditation(/ Stillness)
    - Learning(/ Mind)
    - Artistic(/ Emotional)
- Intensity is how strong the energy is / how strongly you feel that emotion.
- Positive / negative is how better / challenging that energy / emotion is.

- Certain places how open / closed it is makes us feel a certain way.
- Certain people / traits of them makes us feel a certain way.
- Certain time of the whole 24 hours and the time of months make us feel a certain way.
- Overarching structure influences the structure of its details.

Ex: Sports may be a physical activity,

But some people play it for the love of it.

Some may play it to uniquely impact the world through it.

And, some may play it strategically

Ex 2: Home is the 'Ground' filled with emotions:

But some people are caring for / emotionally conflicting each other in it.

Some may be actively switching where they live.

And some people at home may be fighting / healthily passionate about it.

Soul:

Intuitively understanding it.

Soul is a metric of positive and negative. Positivity is a better way to live.

Soul is helping humanity and us to survive more and better.

Injustice and negativity would end life on earth without a soul.

So, you are given blessings and challenges based on your past life to balance justice, and the Hierarchy of advantages to be received by you to help you and whole humanity survive more and better.

All religions have given massive hope to humanity.

Praying to God can increase your belief through consistency and intensity.

Spirituality can help you understand the intangible elements of the world.

Merely praying to God without positive actions towards all parts of your life is like watching a flower without watering it.

In simple…God works when you work.

Applying the concept of Soul intuitively:

Some emotions of aggression can be manipulative / hurtful to others. But in a positive sense, aggression can help us fight to improve ourselves, or we can share the passion with others by inspiring them.

Happiness can be felt by hurting others or in a positive sense; happiness can be felt by helping others.

KARMA

'KARMA' is just energy transactions.

->Positive thoughts / actions dissolve 'karma' and negative ones keep the chain of karma alive.

Positive thoughts and actions can be directed intentionally to where you want to go, creating a new / healthy karmic pattern.

There's possibly an account of every single thought and action in the world.

“Power of your emotions’

What emotions will get triggered, depends on what stimulus the situation is dependent on our imprints / deep memories (from DNA and childhood, and intense memories).

But when we master life, we can overcome these emotional patterns / we can rise above our emotional patterns. And we have control over what emotions to react to and how positively / better we react.

The point is, it feels like, our confident and powerful emotional state has some unknown control over what we think is out of our control, which works in our favour.

So, it’s better to use this power of confidence and positivity as a possible unknown, unpredictable luck.

WE SEE THE WORLD AS WHO, WE ARE, AND WE GET FROM LIFE WHO WE BECOME. THROUGH STRUCTURE.

CHAPTER 10

USEFUL INSIGHTS

A STATEMENT ENDS A THOUGHT, AND A QUESTION CREATES NEW ONES.

MAKE YOUR SUB-CONSCIOUS MIND YOUR BEST FRIEND.

YOU DESERVE THE BEST MINDSET.

ASKING THE RIGHT QUESTION IS HALF OF THE SOLUTION.

EVERY NEGATIVE THING IN THE WORLD IS TRYING TO GROW / MAKE YOU LEARN SOMETHING.

YOU CAN HAVE A LIFE OF COMFORT, PLEASURES AND HAPPINESS, OR YOU CAN HAVE A LIFE OF PAIN OF GROWTH, SUCCESS AND FULFILMENT.

WHEN YOU LEARN HOW TO THINK AND HOW TO LIVE LIFE, YOU CAN THINK ABOUT ANYTHING PROPERLY AND LEAD ANY LIFE THE WORLD HAS GIVEN YOU.

YOU ARE UNIQUE IN RELATION TO OTHER TRAITS AND OTHER PEOPLE.

FIND OPEN ENDED LOOPS AND TRY TO CLOSE THEM TO BECOME INTERESTED IN ANYONE / ANY SKILL / ANYTHING.

PLEASURE PLEASES THE SENSES; BEAUTY PLEASES THE DEEPER PARTS OF YOU.

LOVING SOMEONE IS GIVING WHAT THEY WANT, NOT WHAT YOU THINK THEY NEED AND WANT.

THE BEST WAY TO LIVE IS IN THE CONSTANT PAIN OF GROWTH, WHICH FULFILS YOU POSITIVELY.

YOU DON'T GET STRONGER BECAUSE OF STRUGGLE. YOU GET STRONGER, WHEN YOU ARE HEALING FROM THAT STRUGGLE.

EVERYONE IS THE MAIN CHARACTER IN THEIR LIFE, LIKE YOU ARE IN YOURS.

SELF MASTERY IS A JOURNEY WHERE YOU CAN FIND TREASURES THAT ARE BEYOND YOUR IMAGINATION.

THE INTENSITY OF YOUR FEELINGS DOESN'T ALWAYS GUARANTEE THE RESULTS.

YOU CAN ALWAYS GET WHAT YOU WANT BY DOING WHAT IT TAKES. IF YOU HAVE DONE WHAT IT TAKES, BUT YOU DON'T GET IT. THEN THERE IS ROOM TO IMPROVE, OR IT IS IMPOSSIBLE TO GET IT IN REALITY'S STRUCTURE.

YOUR THOUGHTS, BELIEFS AND ACTIONS ARE POWERFUL WHEN THEY ARE CLOSER TO REALITY.

YOUR MIND WILL BE POWERFUL AND IN AN EXCEPTIONAL STATE WHEN IT'S CONSTANTLY RE ESTABLISHING THE CONNECTION BETWEEN YOU AND REALITY.

ALL DESIRES ARE EXPECTATIONS OF YOU RECEIVING SOME SORT OF VALUE.

YOU ONLY GET HURT WHEN YOU ARE ATTACHED TO SOMETHING.

YOU ARE BUILT TO SURVIVE. SURVIVING BETTER IS A PERSONAL CHOICE.

DISCOVERY -> DO NOT GET LOST IN OPINIONS. EVEN IF IT FEELS EXTREMELY PLEASING / BITTER. DEVELOP THE SKILL OF FINDING THE TRUTH AND STRUCTURE OF REALITY ON YOUR OWN. THERE ARE MANY MYSTERIES IN YOURSELF AND IN THE THE WORLD WHICH NEED YOUR DISCOVERY.

AN EXTREMELY POSITIVE AND EXTREMELY POWERFUL MINDSET IS THE STRONGEST LUXURY THERE IS.

SET THE GOAL, THEN REASON BACKWARDS TO CONNECT THE GOAL TO YOUR CURRENT REALITY, AND UNDERSTAND HOW TO REACH IT.

REALITY IS NOT YOUR EGO, IT'S NOT MY EGO. IT'S NOBODY'S. IT HAS A LIFE OF ITS OWN. AND WE ARE POWERFUL THE CLOSER WE ARE TO IT.

FEEL ALL THE EMOTIONS DEEP FROM YOUR SOUL. BE AS PRACTICAL AS YOU CAN. TAKE EXTREME POSITIVE HEALTHY ACTIONS FROM YOUR SOUL. PUSH YOUR LIMITS SO FAR THAT EVERYONE STARTS TO THINK YOU'RE CRAZY. THIS DOESN'T MAKE YOU THAT CRAZY. IT ONLY GIVES YOU PASSION, LESSONS AND CREATES MORE ROOM TO FEEL LIFE INSIDE OF YOU.

YOU DON'T NEED TO MATCH YOUR INTELLECT TO BE FRIENDS WITH SOMEBODY. YOU NEED AN EMOTIONAL CONNECTION.

FIGHT ALL THE BATTLES THAT YOU NEED TO, BUT DON'T FORGET TO HAVE LOVE INSIDE OF YOU.

HAVING A POINT OF REFERENCE OF THE DEEPEST AND HIGHEST PERCEPTION, CONNECTING BIG IDEAS TO THE DETAILS OF THE PRESENT MOMENT ARE SOURCE OF HIGH PRODUCTIVITY.

LOOK AROUND.
LIFE IS GREAT.
IF IT'S NOT,
MAKE IT GREAT.

YOUR LEVEL OF CONFIDENCE
COMES FROM THE LEVEL
OF MOUNTAINS YOU HAVE
SUCCESSFULLY CLIMBED.

THROUGHOUT YOUR LIFE, YOU WILL
LEARN THREE TYPES OF THINGS.

1) STRUCTURE OF THE WORLD.
2) STRUCTURE OF MANKIND'S CREATION AND MEASUREMENT OF THE WORLD.
3) VALUABLE SKILLS AND TECHNICAL SKILLS THAT CONNECT #1&#2.

YOU FIND PEACE WHEN YOU BECOME NON-REACTIVE AND LET GO OF THE THINGS YOU CAN'T CONTROL. YOU GROW / LEARN MORE BY FINDING AND EXECUTING WHAT IS IN YOUR CONTROL.

RESPECT OTHERS BECAUSE THEY MAY BE RIGHT. RESPECT YOURSELF BECAUSE YOU MAY BE RIGHT. PROVE TO SEE WHO IS ACTUALLY RIGHT WITH RESPECT.

TO ATTRACT EVERYONE, YOU NEED TO HAVE HEAVEN RIGHT WHERE YOU ARE.

EVERYONE IS LUCKY WITH SOMETHING. YOU JUST HAVE TO IDENTIFY IT, AMPLIFY IT, AND USE IT TO YOUR ADVANTAGE.

THE MORE YOU BECOME AWARE OF WHAT IS IN YOUR CONTROL, THE MORE YOU REALISE THAT YOUR CONTROL IN THE WORLD IS GROWING.

YOUR FLAWS AND MISTAKES ARE YOUR GREATEST OPPORTUNITIES BECAUSE YOU GET AN IMMENSE AMOUNT OF FULFILMENT WHEN YOU MAKE IT POSITIVE THROUGH EFFORT.

YOU DON'T HAVE TO WORK HARD.
YOU DON'T HAVE TO WORK SMART.
YOU JUST HAVE TO DO WHAT IT TAKES.

"ROME WAS NOT BUILT IN A DAY.
BUT THEY WERE LAYING BRICKS EVERY HOUR".

JUST GET 1% BETTER CONSTANTLY.

WHEN YOU EXPECT SOMETHING AND THE RESULTS EXCEED IN A NEGATIVE WAY, YOU FEEL SAD. WHEN IT EXCEEDS IN A POSITIVE WAY, YOU'RE HAPPY. WHEN THE RESULT HURTS YOU AND YOU ARE DEFENSIVE, YOU GET ANGRY. WHEN THE RESULT EXCEEDS IN A WAY THAT HURTS YOU AND YOU ARE SUBMISSIVE, YOU FEEL FEAR.

A SOURCE OF GREAT POWER IS EMPATHY. WHERE YOU HAVE THE ABILITY TO FORGET YOURSELF AND FEEL HOW THE OTHER IDEA / PERSON THINKS AND FEELS.

YOU CAN CHANGE IN TWO WAYS; ASSERTION AND TRANSFORMATION

THERE ARE 2 KINDS OF PAIN:

1) DESTRUCTIVE PAIN
2) PAIN OF GROWTH

DESTRUCTIVE PAIN BECOMES PAIN OF GROWTH WHEN YOU CHOOSE TO LEARN FROM IT.

LIFE IS UNFAIR, BUT THE MORE YOU TRY TO UNDERSTAND WHY IT IS THAT WAY. THE MORE YOU MAKE IT FAIR FOR YOURSELF.

IMAGINATION / CONFUSION / ILLUSIONS CAN GET YOU LOST. REALITY WILL MAKE YOU FIND YOURSELF.

"EYE ON THE PRIZE".

UNLEARN, LEARN AND RE-LEARN. TO GET BETTER AND REACH YOUR GOAL.

WINNERS ARE SEPARATED FROM OTHERS BY THEIR "QUALITY OF WORK".

MOST PEOPLE ARE ALREADY HURT IN SOME WAY, SO DON'T BOTHER WHEN THEY DON'T CARE. BE A PERSON OF VALUE SO THAT THEY COME TO YOU FOR VALUE.

ENVY IS JUST NEGATIVE ADMIRATION. KEEP SHOWING THEM REASONS THROUGH RESULTS FOR WHY PEOPLE SHOULD ADMIRE YOU.

"HOW CAN I?"

GOD'S PATH IS THE BEST PATH. IT REQUIRES DISCIPLINE. BUT IGNORANCE CAN CONFUSE YOU THAT IT'S NEGATIVE.

FOCUS ON WHERE YOU ACTUALLY WANT TO GO MORE THAN WHERE YOU DON'T WANT TO GO.

REFLECTING ON YOUR ACTIONS IS AN INVALUABLE SKILL IN THE LEARNING PROCESS.

"SOMETIMES A MOMENT'S INSIGHT IS WORTH A LIFETIME OF EXPERIENCE".

IF YOU ARE CHOOSING TRUE POSITIVITY AND LOVE...AND THE WORLD DOESN'T SUPPORT YOU, THEN STOP CARING ABOUT THE WORLD. IT IS YOU AGAINST THE WORLD TO MAKE YOUR TRUE POSITIVITY WIN.

ALL THAT YOU HAVE TO LIVE THE LIFE THAT YOU WANT IS "RIGHT NOW"- THE PRESENT MOMENT.

SOMETIMES, ALL YOU NEED IS A DIFFERENT PERCEPTION.

FIND YOUR ELEMENT / CREATE ONE.

JUST DO YOUR THING.

YOU CAN CONQUER ALMOST ANY STORM AS LONG AS YOU ARE CALM.

"JUST GIVE ME RESPECT BECAUSE I DESERVE THIS".

CIVILIZATION IS A WORTHY SACRIFICE OF YOUR FREEDOM FOR AN ABUNDANCE OF RESOURCES WHICH CAN MAKE YOU SURVIVE BETTER. BUT NEVER FORGET THAT FREEDOM YOUR SOUL HAS.

CHANNEL YOUR AGGRESSION AND YOUR DARK SIDE INTO WORK.

YOUR GOALS ARE CLOSER FROM INTENSITY OF FOCUS AND FURTHER AWAY FROM DISTRACTIONS.

TRUE STRENGTH IS UNSHAKABLE POSITIVITY.

HALF OF MEDITATION IS FOCUSING ON ONE TASK, AND OTHER HALF IS TO BRING YOUR ATTENTION BACK WHEN YOU LOSE FOCUS.

A FEELING-> MY LIFE IS PERFECT JUST THE WAY IT IS.

THOUGHTS AND EMOTIONS MAY LIE, BUT ACTIONS AND RESULTS DON'T.

GREAT THERAPISTS MAKE YOU LEARN TO THINK.

YOU MAY LACK RESOURCES. BUT YOU CAN ALWAYS BE RESOURCEFUL.

KILL YOUR EGO, AND FEEL THE WHOLE WORLD INSIDE YOU.

EVERY CHALLENGE I CONQUER, LIKE IT'S A MONSTER, BECOMES MY MEDAL OF HONOUR.

MAYBE REALITY EXISTS TO FEEL GOD THROUGH STRUCTURE.

WHEN YOU DON'T COMMIT TO A LIFE OF GROWTH. YOU HAVE ALREADY COMMITTED TO A LIFE OF DECAY.

MY FRIEND, YOU SHOULD STOP CARING ABOUT A FEW THINGS.

THINK OF YOUR MIND AS JUST A MACHINE HELPING YOU SURVIVE. IT HELPS REMOVE EMOTIONS TO MAKE BETTER DECISIONS.

MAKE YOUR CORE THE STRONGEST, SO THAT NOTHING CAN SHAKE YOU.

YOU CAN KEEP WANTING SOMETHING YOUR WHOLE LIFE, OR YOU CAN BE SATISFIED WITH WHAT YOU HAVE (GRATITUDE).

WE ARE SENSITIVE TO NEGATIVITY MORE THAN POSITIVITY BECAUSE POSITIVITY IN OUR PRIMAL BRAIN MEANT WE WOULD LIVE ANOTHER DAY. BUT NEGATIVE THREAT WOULD KILL US RIGHT IN THAT MOMENT.

"INTEREST" IS THE EMOTION WHICH DRIVES US WHEN WE ARE RECEIVING VALUE.

IT FEELS LIKE IN THE PROCESS OF BECOMING SUCCESSFUL YOU ARE CLEANSED FROM NEGATIVITY AND ONLY YOUR POSITIVE SELF IS LEFT TO ENJOY THE FRUITS OF YOUR LABOUR.

BETTER DESIRES ARE CLOSER TO GOD.

I'M NAKED IN GOD'S WORLD.

ANY AREA OF LIFE WHERE
EMOTIONS HAVE TO BE SPARKED
FOR A GOAL, IT BECOMES AN "ART".

HOW TO THINK 3 STEPS AHEAD:

1) BE SELF AWARE AND AWARE
2) LEARN FROM PAST PATTERNS
3) TRY PREDICTING FUTURE PATTERNS
4) (REFLECT LATER)

STRUGGLES CAN BECOME LESSONS AND LESSONS CAN BECOME SUCCESSES.

WHAT YOU DO WHEN YOU ARE NOT WORKING IS IMPORTANT FOR YOUR WORK TOO.

THE POWER OF FAME ->NOVELTY OF VALUE.
PROPORTION / SIZE OF FAME-> ACCESSIBILITY OF THAT VALUE TO THE NUMBER OF PEOPLE.

YOU MAY HAVE BEEN DEALT A BAD HAND. THAT IS NOT AN EXCUSE TO BE NEGATIVE. EXTRAORDINARY THINGS CAN COME TO YOU WHEN YOU ACCEPT YOUR FATE AND MAKE THE MOST OUT OF IT.

GROUNDING: SIT IN SILENCE AND DO NOTHING FOR A FEW MOMENTS A DAY. LET YOUR MIND FLOW LIKE A RIVER, BY NOT ENGAGING IN IT.

TO GIVE WHAT THE WORLD WANTS THROUGH YOUR ELEMENT.

DON'T BE LIFELESS AND PASSIVE. PLANTS DON'T GROW WITHOUT RAIN. LOVE DOESN'T BLOOM WITHOUT ATTENTION, AND SUCCESS CAN'T HAPPEN WITHOUT ACTION.

REAL LUCK IS IN YOUR MINDSET. LUCK IS DISCOVERING POSITIVITY WHERE IT FEELS LIKE IT'S NOT THERE. IT MAY HAPPEN ONCE, OR IT CAN BE A TRAIT.

IMAGINARY BELIEF IS CRAZY. BELIEF CLOSER TO REALITY IS PRODUCTIVE.

ONE MAN'S HYPER CALCULATED ACTION IS BLIND LUCK TO THE IGNORANT MAN.

JUSTICE IS A RIGHT. FOR SOME, IT'S A RESPONSIBILITY.

PEOPLE RESPECT YOUR GOOD TRAITS MORE WHEN YOU HAVE MORE VALUE.

TRAITS CAN BE INHERITED. BUT EXCELLENCE HAS TO BE EARNED.

THANK YOU, GOD.

EXCELLENCE:

EVERYONE WANTS LOVE, AND SOME PEOPLE CREATE DRAMA TO GET IT. IF YOU REACT BADLY TO THEIR DRAMA, THEN YOU ARE AUTOMATICALLY THE BAD PERSON.

YOUR PRESENT SITUATION WILL MAKE PERFECT SENSE TO THE PERCEPTION OF YOUR "BEST SELF".

I AM SORRY FOR ALL THE MISTAKES I HAVE MADE.

EVERYTHING IN THIS WORLD CAN BE MEASURED.

DISCIPLINE IS TRAINING YOUR MIND TO THINK, FEEL AND ACT IN A CERTAIN WAY.

IF GOD SAYS "JUMP OFF A CLIFF", I'M JUMPING OFF A CLIFF. BUT THE CHALLENGE IS TO UNDERSTAND IF GOD IS SPEAKING / IF NEGATIVITY IS.

GOD WILL ANSWER YOUR PRAYERS. IN THE WAY OF POSITIVITY. NOT IN THE WAY YOU WANT IT TO BE. THE SECRET IS BELIEVING AND LETTING GO OF YOUR PRAYERS.

ONE OF THE BIGGEST CHALLENGES IN LIFE IS, GETTING THE "RIGHT INFORMATION".

"MASTERY" STATE OF MIND.

INTELLIGENT PEOPLE DON'T HAVE AN ADVANTAGE TO BEING SUCCESSFUL. BECAUSE THEY CAN EASILY STUCK IN CONFUSIONS, OR THEY CAN BECOME LAZY.

"STRATEGY"

HUSTLER'S STRUGGLES:

- Building skills
  - losing relatability between other people and themselves.
  - change of values / principles
  - Envy from others
  - Constant state of being in destructive pain and pain of growth.

SOLUTION:

Self-reliance, strength, work and powerful mindset.

ENVY:

YOUR MERE EXISTENCE WHEN YOU ARE SUCCESSFUL TRIGGERS ENVY IN OTHERS. YOU NEED A STRONG STRATEGY TO DEAL WITH PEOPLE.

DESIRE:

IF YOU REALLY WANT NOTHING, YOU'LL BE A BEGGAR; IF YOU REALLY WANT GOD AND NOTHING ELSE, YOU'LL BE A SAINT; IF YOU REALLY WANT TO LEARN, YOU WILL BE ABUNDANT.

YOU NEED ENERGY TO LIVE AND YOU DON'T NEED ENERGY IF YOU WANT TO DIE. THAT IS WHY PAIN OF GROWTH FEELS LIGHT AND PAIN OF DECAY FEELS HEAVY. ONE IS TRYING TO MAKE YOU LIVE MORE. ANOTHER IS TRYING TO KILL YOU MORE.

ALMOST EVERY PHYSICAL WORLD'S SCENARIOS ARE LIKE CARDS BEING DEALT TO STRENGTHEN YOUR IMMATERIAL MIND.

ALL OF MY QUOTES ARE TOOLS / POINTS OF REFERENCE TO FIND YOUR OWN UNIQUE TRUTH.